For my two girls, Aurora and Madison
who like every girl and boy,
are wonderfully and extraordinarily unique.

Text Copyright: Jodie A Eaton 2017 ©
Illustration Copyright: Jodie A Eaton 2017 ©
All rights reserved

ISBN-13: 978-1543270648
ISBN-10: 1543270646

Jodie A Eaton has asserted her right to be identified as the author and illustrator of this work under the copyright,
designs and patent act, 1988

What Makes You, You?

This pony is unique...

...this lizard is very different...

...and this woman is extraordinary!

Although they may not look it, they are similar to one another.

They each have something which makes them unique, different and extraordinary.

The pony is actually a unicorn!
She was born with a magical and beautiful horn.

Her horn makes her different to all the other ponies,

but also makes her extraordinarily wonderful!

The lizard is actually a chameleon!
Unlike other lizards it has the ability to
display beautiful colours which help it blend
into its surroundings.

This ability makes
it extraordinary,

but also wonderfully unique.

The woman is a Paralympian!

She was born with one leg and uses a special blade to run. She has won an Olympic medal for her country!

Simply extraordinary!

This achievement makes her wonderfully different and unique.

This is George, Aurora and Charlie.

Just like the unicorn, chameleon and Paralympian these three people each have something different about them.

Can you guess what it is?

George was born with no eyes and cannot see.

It makes him look a bit different.

Aurora was born with a small eye, which she cannot see out of.

It makes her look a bit different.

Charlie was born with a condition in one eye called coloboma.

It makes him look a bit different.

Some of us are born with something that makes us different.

This makes us extraordinary and wonderfully unique.

When you think about it...

...isn't everyone different, unique and extraordinary in their own way?

No two people are the same!

What makes you different, makes you...

...YOU!

George, Aurora and Charlie could feel sad or question why they look different.

Sometimes people can say silly things or leave them out of games, because they don't understand about their differences.

It is important to realise that looking different is a *PART* of who you are, not *WHO* you are.

Having friends around that appreciate our differences, accept that we are unique and love that we are wonderfully extraordinary, is what helps everyone to be happy being themselves.

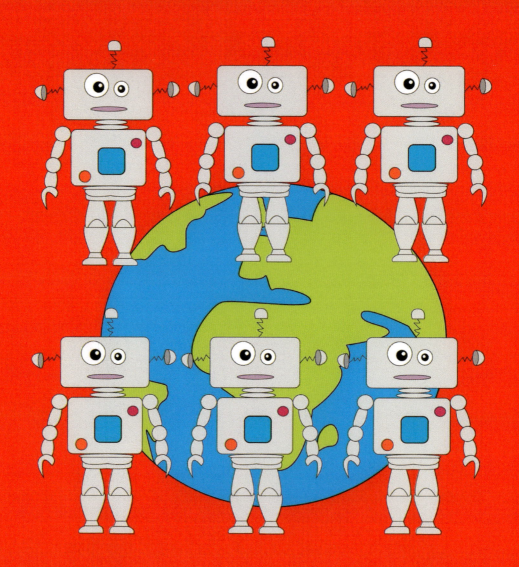

If we all looked the same the world would be a very boring place...

...don't you think?

So this is for the different ones,
the Georges, Auroras and Charlies,
the unicorns, chameleons and Paralympians!

In fact, this is a message for anyone in the world who has something that makes them unique, different and wonderfully extraordinary.

Remember, everybody views the world differently.

You may be different,
but you *are*
extraordinarily and wonderfully unique

and what is best, best of all… Is that you are…

YOU

And in case you need reminding...

"Be yourself, everyone else is already taken" *Oscar Wilde*

"By being yourself you put something wonderful in the world that was not there before" *Edwin Elliot*

"Being different isn't a bad thing, it means you are brave enough to be yourself"

Luna Lovegood

"Different is good, when someone tells you that you are different, smile, hold your head up and be proud"

Angelina Jolie

"The things that make me different are the things that make me" *Winnie The Pooh*

Printed in Great Britain
by Amazon